Before reading this book, the rea

· two or more letters can represen

· the spelling <oo> can represent the _____ __

This book introduces:

· the spelling <oo> for the sound 'oo' as in 'boot'
· text at CVCCC and CCVC level

High-frequency words:

look, this, says, is, a, the, hold, does, this, to, holds, as, they, have, so

Vocabulary:

mood – the way someone feels
zoom – to move very quickly
noon – twelve o'clock midday

Talk about the story:

Have you ever been in a bad mood?
What do you do to snap out of it?
Find out what Nan does when she
is in a bad mood…

Reading Practice

Practise blending these sounds into words:

t oo

b oo t

r oo f

f oo d

m oo n

br oo m

sp oo n

Zoom!

"Look at this room!" Nan says.

Nan is in a bad mood.

Cat is in a bad mood too.

"Let's get on the mop and zoom from the room," says Nan.

Vroom!

"Hold on!" yells Nan.

The mop does a loop the loop.

"This is cool," says Nan.

"Let's zoom up onto the roof!"

says Nan. Vroom!

The mop zooms onto the roof.

"Let's zoom up to the moon!"
says Nan. Cat holds on as
they zoom to the moon.

Soon it is noon.

Nan and Cat have food on

the moon. So cool!

Questions for discussion:

- Why was Nan in a bad mood?

- How would you feel if you flew to the moon?

- If you could fly on a magic mop, where would you go?

Game with <oo> words

Play as pelmanism or use for reading practice. Enlarge and
photocopy the page twice on two different colours of card.
Cut the cards up to play.
Ensure the players sound out the words.

boot	zoom	moon
room	cool	root
food	mood	roof
too	hoof	noon